DATE DUE

		MAR 1 4 2015	
			JUN 2 5 2016
			PRINTED IN U.S.A.

POP CULTURE BIOS

JADEN

SMITH

CHILDREN'S ROOM

ACTOR, RAPPER, AND ACTIVIST

BY HEATHER E. SCHWARTZ

Lerner Publications Company

MINNEAPOLIS

Thank you to Nolan Schwartz, a
superstar son who gave me the
time I needed to write this book.

Lerner Publications Company
A division of Lerner Publishing Group, Inc.
241 First Avenue North
Minneapolis, MN 55401 USA

For reading levels and more information, look up this title at
www.lernerbooks.com.

Library of Congress Cataloging-in-Publication Data

Schwartz, Heather E.
      Jaden Smith : actor, rapper, and activist / by Heather E.
   Schwartz.
         p.   cm — (Pop culture bios)
      Includes index.
      ISBN 978–1–4677–1441–9 (lib. bdg. : alk. paper)
      ISBN 978–1–4677–2500–2 (eBook)
      1. Smith, Jaden, 1998— Juvenile literature. 2. Actors—
   United States—Biography—Juvenile literature. I. Title.
   PN2287.S6125S39 2014
   791.4302'8092—dc23[B]   2013018362

Manufactured in the United States of America
1 – PC – 12/31/13

INTRODUCTION

Jaden attends a movie premiere with some family members. Pictured here (FROM LEFT): Jaden, Will Smith, Jada Pinkett Smith, and Willow Smith.

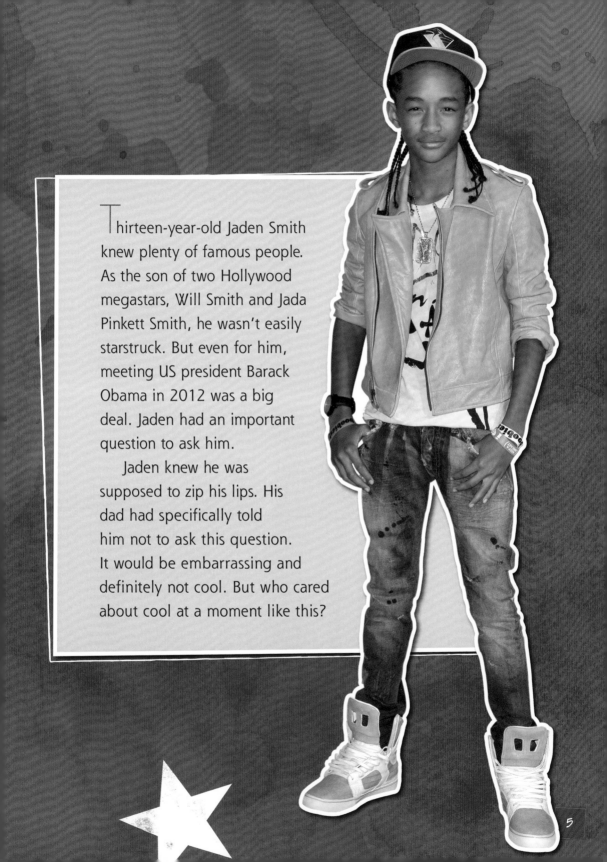

Thirteen-year-old Jaden Smith knew plenty of famous people. As the son of two Hollywood megastars, Will Smith and Jada Pinkett Smith, he wasn't easily starstruck. But even for him, meeting US president Barack Obama in 2012 was a big deal. Jaden had an important question to ask him.

Jaden knew he was supposed to zip his lips. His dad had specifically told him not to ask this question. It would be embarrassing and definitely not cool. But who cared about cool at a moment like this?

The president was giving Jaden and his family a private tour of the White House. They'd just reached the Situation Room, where top secret meetings are held. It was now or never.

With a glint in his eye, Jaden did it. He told the president that he wanted to know the truth about aliens. President Obama said he couldn't officially confirm that aliens were real. But he also didn't say they weren't real. That was proof enough for Jaden!

Jaden was in awe when he met President Barack Obama in 2012.

So what if he came off as less than cool? Jaden wasn't the kind of kid to miss out on opportunities. When they came his way, he jumped to grab them. That was how he'd landed movie roles. That was how he'd started rapping. That was how he'd become a star in his own right, instead of just the son of famous parents.

And now he had his answer about aliens—from the commander in chief himself!

Jaden demonstrates his rapping skills. Rapping is just one of Jaden's many talents.

Jaden poses for a pic with his parents and little sis.

CHAPTER ONE

BORN FAMOUS

Will and Jada, shown here when Jada was pregnant with Jaden, are both Hollywood legends.

In some ways, Jaden Christopher Syre Smith is just like any other kid. He hangs with his friends. He loves to skateboard in his spare time. His little sister bugs him. But for the most part, his life is far from normal.

With major movie stars for parents, Jaden was in the spotlight before he was even born. When he was still only a bump in his mom's belly, he appeared in his dad's music video, "Just the Two of Us." His birthday—July 8, 1998—was ginormous news.

SPOTLIGHT ON SIBLINGS

Jaden's younger sister, Willow (RIGHT, WITH JADEN), is a performer too. Their older half brother, Trey Smith, is a DJ. Jaden's close to both of them...even though Willow bosses him around a lot.

For the first few years of his life, Jaden flew under the radar. But when he was six, his parents took on a new project. They created and produced their own sitcom, *All of Us*. There was a part for a little boy in six of the episodes. Hey, Jaden…you're on!

Jaden, eight years old, gets a piggyback ride from his dad.

The Pursuit of a Movie Role

Some people said Jaden's parents pushed him into show biz. But even as a little guy, Jaden had a mind of his own. Case in point: One night, his dad was reading a script for a new movie, *The Pursuit of Happyness*. His dad was going to play a man with a young son. Lightbulb! Seven-year-old Jaden had a great idea. Why couldn't he play the son?

TOO COOL FOR SCHOOL

Jaden's parents believe in homeschooling, so he's never been to school. He's taught by private tutors instead. His favorite subject: math.

Jaden, around the time he was chosen to act in *The Pursuit of Happyness*.

The role wasn't cast yet, so Jaden got a shot at the part. Out of more than one hundred boys, he won the role. Sure, being the real son of the lead actor didn't hurt. But the filmmakers really believed he was the best of the bunch. They thought he had talent. On set, Jaden set out to prove them right.

LEAD =
the star, or the person with the biggest role

Jaden wowed audiences and critics in his debut movie, *The Pursuit of Happyness*.

At the 2007 Oscars, Jaden got up onstage as an award presenter. But for him, the most memorable part of the night was the after-party. That's where he met his favorite actress, Sarah Michelle Gellar. He was so excited he couldn't say a word!

Jaden and fellow young actor Abigail Breslin presented an award at the Oscars.

Workin' the Tears

He did have some experience already. Plus, his dad was by his side. Still, acting in a movie wasn't a no-brainer for Jaden. This was a much bigger role than his bit part on *All of Us*. He had lots of lines to learn. He was in tons of scenes. He even had to cry in front of the camera. At first, Jaden couldn't cry on command. But then he remembered his dad's advice: he had to really feel what his character was feeling instead of just pretending. So he started thinking sad thoughts, and the tears flowed.

The filmmakers were impressed. His father was blown away. After the movie came out in 2006, critics raved about Jaden's acting. Jaden even won an MTV Movie Award for Best Breakthrough Performance.

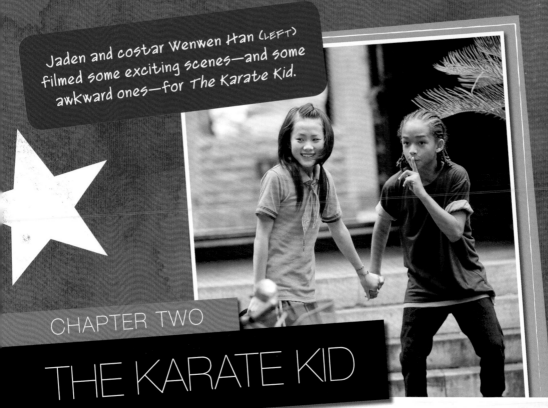

Jaden and costar Wenwen Han (LEFT) filmed some exciting scenes—and some awkward ones—for The Karate Kid.

CHAPTER TWO

THE KARATE KID

Jaden tested his martial arts skills with one of the best fighters in show biz: Jackie Chan (LEFT).

When Jaden was ten, he added hip-hop dance to his list of talents. After just five days of lessons, he could move like a pro. He proved it on *The Ellen DeGeneres Show*, when he visited to talk about his latest movie, *The Day the Earth Stood Still*. In between laughing and joking with him, Ellen praised Jaden's acting skills. His career was taking off.

Jaden's next movie, *The Karate Kid*, was his biggest yet. He briefly busted out his dance moves in the film. But that wasn't the only skill he showed off. Before filming, he spent three months training in martial arts. Then the whole family headed off to China. There, Jaden trained three hours a day for another four months.

MARTIAL ARTS =
a type of sport with special fighting techniques

But his biggest challenge turned out to be the kissing scene. Jaden had his first on-screen smooch with costar Wenwen Han—while his parents were on set!

How did he handle it? He made sure that security at least kept his mom away! Still, getting the kiss right took more than thirty-two takes. And these weren't romantic moments for eleven-year-old Jaden. Even between takes, Jaden and Wenwen had to stand next to each other with their faces just inches apart. Talk about awkward!

All the hard work paid off, though. When *The Karate Kid* hit theaters, Jaden's performance made him an instant idol. At the movie premiere, reporters focused their attention on the young star—not just his parents. In June 2010, *J-14* magazine named him the Hot Guy of the Week.

CHA-CHING!

After making *The Karate Kid*, Jaden became Hollywood's highest-paid child actor. He earned more than $3 million for the film.

Jaden shows off a martial arts move at the German premiere of *The Karate Kid*.

He was used to being part of a famous family. He was even used to attention from girls. But this was something new.

MASTER FAN

Action movie legend Jackie Chan, who starred with Jaden in *The Karate Kid*, was wowed by how hard Jaden worked and how fast he learned. Chan even joked that he'd like to adopt Jaden. And he predicted that if Jaden kept training, he could be a major martial arts star.

Soon Jaden couldn't go anywhere without getting mobbed by fans and journalists. But he quickly learned to fly under the radar. If he wore a hood, looked straight ahead, and didn't stop to chat, few people actually recognized him.

BONDING WITH BIEBER

Jaden got tight with pop sensation Justin Bieber when they recorded the theme song for *The Karate Kid*. On "Never Say Never," Jaden rapped and Justin sang. They sounded so good together that they later recorded another song, "Happy New Year."

Giving Back

With the world's attention on him, Jaden could use his famous name to get pretty much whatever he wanted. And what this kid wanted was a chance to help.

In 2009, he connected with Project Zambi. The organization helps African orphans whose parents have died of AIDS. Jaden and his sister, Willow, became youth ambassadors for Project Zambi. That meant speaking out to get attention for the cause. It also meant donating his autograph. He signed a model of an elephant—a common animal in many parts of Africa—that Project Zambi then auctioned off on eBay. Money from the elephant's sale went straight to the orphans.

Jaden and Willow (RIGHT) team up to help orphans in Africa.

WILL SMITH   JADEN SMITH

DANGER IS REAL   FEAR IS A CHOICE

AFTER EARTH
12A

COLUMBIA PICTURES PRESENTS AN OVERBROOK ENTERTAINMENT/BLINDING EDGE PICTURES PRODUCTION A FILM BY M. NIGHT SHYAMALAN "AFTER EARTH"
CASTING ASHWIN RAJAN, JOHN ROSK MUSIC JAMES NEWTON HOWARD COSTUME AMY WESTCOTT EDITOR JONATHAN BOTHBART PRODUCTION STEVEN ROSENBURN A.C.E.
DESIGN TOM SANDERS PHOTOGRAPHY PETER SUSCHITZKY A.S.C. PRODUCERS E. BENNETT WALSH EXECUTIVE WILL SMITH SCREENPLAY GARY WHITTA AND M. NIGHT SHYAMALAN
PRODUCED CALEB PINKETT, JADA PINKETT SMITH & WILL SMITH, JAMES LASSITER, M. NIGHT SHYAMALAN DIRECTED M. NIGHT SHYAMALAN

www.afterearth.co.uk   afterearthmovie #afterearth

OPENS JUNE 7

on the go, by phone or in cinema
.uk / 08 714 714 714   EMPIRE CINEMAS

CHAPTER THREE

SOLO ACT

Jaden sports his designer streetwear while skateboarding.

Jaden raps with his dad in Miami, Florida.

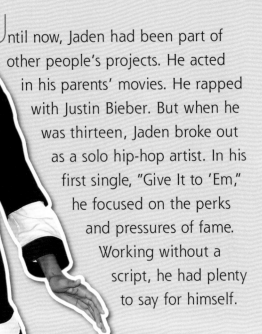

Until now, Jaden had been part of other people's projects. He acted in his parents' movies. He rapped with Justin Bieber. But when he was thirteen, Jaden broke out as a solo hip-hop artist. In his first single, "Give It to 'Em," he focused on the perks and pressures of fame. Working without a script, he had plenty to say for himself.

SCRIPT =
the written text of a movie, a show, or another performance

Jaden's dad, Will, says he doesn't pry too much into Jaden's life. But Jaden says he stays open with his father. He's convinced that Will always knows what he's up to anyway—even if Will won't admit it! And when Will caught Jaden skateboarding inside their house in May of 2013, you can bet Dad had something to say about it!

Jaden insisted he didn't care what others thought of his work. He just wanted to express his thoughts and feelings honestly.

Soon he released a whole collection of songs called *The Cool Café: Cool Tape Volume 1*. Each track gave listeners a glimpse into his head.

Solo Style

Jaden had his own album, so why not his own look? In 2013, he launched a clothing line called MSFtS (pronounced "misfits"). He chose the name because he'd always felt different. He wanted to reach out to others who felt as though they didn't fit in with the mainstream.

He decided that MSFtS clothing should be unusual and surprising—just like him.

Willow (LEFT) helps promote her brother's fashion line.

23

So how did fashionistas feel about it? At least one became a fan. In early 2013, teen model Kylie Jenner wore some MSFtS duds for a night on the town. But everyone wanted to know: Was she just in love with the MSFtS style? Or was her heart set on Jaden?

Kylie dons a MSFtS shirtdress for the 2013 Nickelodeon Kids' Choice Awards.

After all, the two had been seen hanging out together more than once.

Jaden told reporters that he had a great relationship with Kylie. He called her one of his best friends. But he wouldn't say whether he and Kylie were more than friends. When it comes to romance, Jaden prefers to keep his private life private!

WORLD TRAVELER

Jaden's touched down in China, Cancun, London, and New York City, to name just a few famous hot spots. His favorite food that he had while in China? Believe it or not, it was a hamburger! It's the simple things that keep Jaden happy.

Jaden traveled to South Korea in 2013 to promote one of his latest films.

Jaden had a major role in *After Earth*. This is the second movie in which Jaden starred with his father.

The Future Looks Cool

Jaden had plenty of projects—and high-profile friendships— to keep him busy. Acting was still a major part of his life, though. He starred in three movies in 2013: *After Earth*, a sci-fi thriller; *The Karate Kid 2*, the sequel to his biggest film; and *Amulet*, based on the first book of a fantasy series.

So what does the future hold for a kid who can act, rap, dance, and even design clothing? Will Jaden keep acting? What about his music career?

He's definitely working on a second album. But he also says he's taking it easy for now. And why not? At fifteen, Jaden has plenty of time to decide how he'll wow fans next.

HOME SWEET HOME

Rumor had it that Jaden wanted to get his own place when he turned fifteen. True? Not! Jaden says he doesn't plan on leaving the family home anytime soon. He and his dad made a deal: Jaden will move out only if he makes a movie that's bigger than any of Will's movies!

JADEN
★ PICS!

Jaden and Willow (LEFT) put on some bling for the 2011 Nickelodeon Kids' Choice Awards.

MORE JADEN INFO

Doeden, Matt. *Will Smith*. Minneapolis: Lerner Publications, 2007. Read about Jaden's famous dad, from his early days on the 1990s sitcom *The Fresh Prince of Bel-Air* to his music career, acting, and family life.

Gosman, Gillian. *Jaden Smith*. Mankato, MN: Sea-to-Sea Publications, 2013.
Learn more about Jaden's life story.

Hibbert, Clare. *Jaden Smith*. London: Franklin Watts, 2012.
Read up to feed your Jaden obsession.

Jaden Smith
http://www.jadensmith.com
See what Jaden's up to with these official links to his social networking sites.

Rajczak, Kristen. *Jaden Smith*. New York: Gareth Stevens Publishing, 2012.
Find out more about Jaden's life and career.

Tieck, Sarah. *Jaden Smith*. Edina, MN: Abdo, 2011.
Get the scoop on Jaden—plus lots of photos!

INDEX

PHOTO ACKNOWLEDGMENTS

The images in this book are used with the permission of: © Alexander Tamargo/WireImage/Getty Images, p. 2; © Jeff Kravitz/FilmMagic/Getty Images, p. 3 (top), 10; © D. Dipasupil/FilmMagic/Getty Images, pp. 3 (bottom), 7; © Alexander Tamargo/WireImage/Getty Images, pp. 2, 4 (top); © Gareth Cattermole/Getty Images, p. 4 (bottom); © Paul Smith/FeatureFlash/Shutterstock.com, p. 5; © Saul Loeb/AFP/Getty Images, p. 6; © Mike Nelson/EPA/CORBIS, p. 8 (top); Manuel Munoz/PacificCoast News/Newscom, p. 8 (bottom left); © SGranitz/WireIMage/Getty Images, p. 8 (bottom right); © Kevin Mazur/KCA2013 /WireImage/Getty Images, p. 9; © Stephanie Cardinale/People Avenue/CORBIS, p. 11; © AF Archive/Alamy, p. 12; © Kevin Winter/Getty Images, pp. 13, 18; © Jasin Boland/Columbia /Courtesy Everett Collection, pp. 14 (top), (bottom); © ZumaPress/Alamy, p. 15; Tschirner/ZUMAPress/Newscom, p. 16; © ZUMA Press Inc./Alamy, p. 17; Everett Collection/Newscom, p. 19; © Mim Friday/Alamy, p. 20 (top); Manuel Munoz/Pacific Coast News/Newscom, p. 20 (bottom left); © Gustavo Caballero/Getty Images for Columbia, p. 20 (bottom right); © Tim P. Whitby/Getty Images, p. 21; © Issei Kato/Reuters/CORBIS, p. 22; © Jason LaVeris/FilmMagic/Getty Images, p. 23; © Steve Granitz/WireImage/Getty Images, p. 24; © Jung Yeon-Je/AFP/Getty Images, p. 25; © Sony Pictures/Courtesy Everett Collection, p. 26; © Dimitrios Kambouris/WireImage/Getty Images, p. 27; © S_bukley/ImageCollect, p. 28 (top left); © Imagecollect/Dreamstime.com, p. 28 (bottom left); © Jamie McCarthy/Getty Images for Mercedes-Benz, p. 28 (right); © iStockphoto.com/EdStock, p. 29 (top left); © Skycafemx/Dreamstime.com, p. 29 (bottom left); © S_bukley/Shutterstock.com, p. 29 (right).

Front cover: © Junko Kimura/Jana Press/Zuma/ImageCollect (main); © Dimitrios Kambouris/WireImage/Getty Images.
Back cover: © S_bukley/ImageCollect.

Main body text set in Shannon Std Book 12/18.
Typeface provided by Monotype Typography.